GEARED FOR GROWTH BIBLE STUDIES

THE THRONE AND TEMPLE

A STUDY IN 1 & 2 CHRONICLES

BIBLE STUDIES TO IMPACT THE LIVES
OF ORDINARY PEOPLE

Written by Dorothy Russell

The Word Worldwide

CHRISTIAN FOCUS

For details of our titles visit us on our website
www.christianfocus.com

ISBN 1-85792-910-1

Copyright © WEC International

Published in 2003 by
Christian Focus Publications, Geanies House,
Fearn, Ross-shire, IV20 1TW, Scotland
and
WEC International, Bulstrode, Oxford Road,
Gerrards Cross, Bucks, SL9 8SZ

Cover design by Alister MacInnes

Printed and bound by J W Arrowsmith, Bristol

CONTENTS

PREFACE 4
INTRODUCTORY STUDY 5

QUESTIONS AND NOTES

STUDY 1: FAITH IN THE SAVIOUR 7
STUDY 2: GOD'S EVERLASTING COVENANT 9
STUDY 3: THE KINGDOM OF GOD 11
STUDY 4: WORSHIP 13
STUDY 5: WORSHIP – THE LORD'S RESPONSE 16
STUDY 6: THE KINGDOM DIVIDED 19
STUDY 7: A LESSON IN TRUSTING GOD 22
STUDY 8: WEAKNESS AND STRENGTH 25
STUDY 9: DIVINE JUSTICE – GOD IS NOT MOCKED 27
STUDY 10: RESTORING RELATIONSHIPS 30
STUDY 11: GOD WORKS OUT HIS PURPOSES 33

ANSWER GUIDE

STUDY 1 36
STUDY 2 37
STUDY 3 38
STUDY 4 39
STUDY 5 39
STUDY 6 40
STUDY 7 41
STUDY 8 42
STUDY 9 43
STUDY 10 44
STUDY 11 45

PREFACE
GEARED FOR GROWTH

'Where there's LIFE there's GROWTH:
Where there's GROWTH there's LIFE.'

WHY GROW a study group?

Because as we study the Bible and share together we can

- learn to combat loneliness, depression, staleness, frustration, and other problems
- get to understand and love each other
- become responsive to the Holy Spirit's dealing and obedient to God's Word

and that's GROWTH.

How do you GROW a study group?

- Just start by asking a friend to join you and then aim at expanding your group.
- Study the set portions daily (they are brief and easy: no catches).
- Meet once a week to discuss what you find.
- Befriend others, both Christians and non Christians, and work away together

see how it GROWS!

WHEN you GROW ...

This will happen at school, at home, at work, at play, in your youth group, your student fellowship, women's meetings, mid-week meetings, churches and communities,

you'll be REACHING THROUGH TEACHING

INTRODUCTORY STUDY

Why read the Old Testament (the Hebrew Scriptures) at all? What has such ancient history to do with us today? How can it possibly help us as we consider the future of our world? Perhaps you sometimes wonder about this.

How would you answer someone who asked you these questions? Share your thoughts in your group.

Imagine that it is 400 years before Christ, in the fourth century BC. Almost 200 years ago, Jerusalem with its splendid TEMPLE was totally destroyed, and the last KING and his people brutally led away captive by Nebuchadnezzar.

It is over 100 years since the faithful remnant of the Jews returned to their homeland with Zerubbabel and with Ezra, and then with Nehemiah. But for their descendants, life is grim. They have no king, and the people are under Persian rule. They are well versed in what we now call the books of Samuel and Kings (see 2 Chron. 16:11 and 32:32) which tell of their nation's past.

But why read these Hebrew Scriptures?

What has such ancient history to do with them, in their day? How can it possibly help them as they consider their future?

Let's listen in to a conversation.

HODAVIAH: Our Scriptures tell us of 'the good old days'. It was easy for the people in King David's time, or King Hezekiah's day, to be faithful to the Lord. They had a good leader to look up to. But we have never had a king to govern us and judge us wisely.

AKKUB: Yes, what's the use of reading the Scriptures? We have heard of the wonderful events described in Samuel and Kings, but they only make us realize the contrast between the days of the monarchy and now.

HODAVIAH: God was at work in the world in those days, but those times are past. True, the temple in Jerusalem has been rebuilt, but it is a second-rate thing compared with Solomon's temple, and we, the people of God, are a feeble minority under Persian rule. Sometimes even our priests are corrupt. How can they represent us to God?

AKKUB: I often wonder if we can really claim to be the people of God any longer. Life in our modern secular world is so different from the days of our ancestors. How can our nation's history help us today? Times have changed.

HODAVIAH: I can't see that history is relevant at all. In this day and age we face a bleak future. Where can we turn for help? You and I can both trace our ancestry back to the royal line, but what good is that? There will never be another king of Judah, as far as I can see. Sometimes it seems as if God doesn't care about us any more.

It was at this point in time (the fourth century BC) that the Holy Spirit inspired the Chronicler to take the historical account of God's people, and from it to preach a spiritual message to the discouraged people of his day. Think of these books we are going to study as a sermon presenting divine principles. These principles are true in our own day also, because they are changeless. God still acts in the way that He did in the past, though our circumstances may be different.

One of the themes we can look out for is illustrated by the events mentioned in 1 Chronicles 5:18-26. Read these verses together and discuss what the divine principles are. Do they still apply in our society today?

As we begin our study of 1 Chronicles, your leader will take you quickly through chapters 1–9, to show how the covenant plan of God can be traced from Adam right down to the day when the Chronicler was writing.

Later in our study we shall see how the THRONE and the TEMPLE foreshadow the role of the One who is the King of Kings, and our great High Priest.

All Biblical quotations are from The Holy Bible, New International Version unless otherwise stated.

STUDY 1

FAITH IN THE SAVIOUR

QUESTIONS

DAY 1   *1 Chronicles 10:1-7, 13, 14.*
a) What reasons are given as to why Saul died?
b) What divine principle does this section illustrate?

DAY 2   *1 Chronicles 11:1-9; 12:38-40.*
a) What two roles had the Lord said David would fill?
b) Luke 1:32-33; John 10:11. Who fulfils these roles today?
c) How did David contrast with Saul?

DAY 3   *1 Chronicles 13:1-8.*
a) How did David show he wanted to put God first when he was king?
b) What had not been done in the reign of Saul that David now wanted to put right?

DAY 4   *1 Chronicles 13:9; Luke 6:46.*
a) What did the incident about Uzzah teach the people about God (symbolized by the ark)?
b) Who received the blessing?

DAY 5   *1 Chronicles 14:1-17.*
a) How does this chapter show that Divine grace overrules even after a mistake (13:10) has been made?
b) How far did David's fame spread?

DAY 6   *1 Chronicles 15:1-4, 11-15; Numbers 4:1-6, 15.*
a) What were the 'Maker's instructions' for moving the ark?
b) Look carefully at verse 13. Who did David blame for the Lord's anger against Uzzah?

DAY 7   *1 Chronicles 15:16–16:6.*
a) If you had been watching this joyful celebration, what would you have seen and heard?
b) When the ark had been brought to Jerusalem and set in its place, what new job was given to the Levites?

NOTES

God's plan for a king over His people was for one who would be His representative on earth. We can see how dismally Saul failed in this respect. However the Chronicler shows us David as a man after God's own heart who, though he was not perfect, helped the people to see what God was like. And we, as Christians, can see how Jesus, who was later given 'the throne of His father David', fulfilled perfectly that role of being God's representative on earth.

Have you noticed how much JOY we have been reading about in this study?

Three days of joyous festivities (11:1; 12:38-40)
When David became king 'there was joy in Israel'. It must have been quite a party, as you will see if you glance at the amounts given in chapter 12, and yet there were 'plentiful supplies' for all.
When Christians gather to proclaim Christ as King, there is joy, and a plentiful supply of blessings!

Excitement at the prospect of bringing back the ark (13:3-8)
People came flocking from far and wide to join the procession, which took on the nature of a carnival, with music and singing, and people celebrating with all their might. Then suddenly, into this joyful scene came a jarring note. Uzzah was struck down.
As we celebrate the Lord's presence in our midst, let us always remember that He is a holy God, and He expects due reverence from us as we worship Him.

Three months of blessing for Obed-Edom (13:14)
Although this man was not an Israelite, he had learned that God required respect for the ark, and so he received blessing.
When things are right between God and His people today, we can expect His good hand to be on us.

Rejoicing all the way as the ark is brought to the city
What a thrilling procession that must have been, and how carefully it was organized! Can't you just hear the musicians and the choirs, and see the priests clothed in linen carrying the ark in the prescribed way, and all the people clapping and dancing as they went their way to the city?
God has given us music as a way of expressing our joy at being His people. When we obey what is written in His word, and live our lives according to His pattern, we can experience the truth of Jesus' words: 'If you obey my commands, you will remain in my love ... I have told you this so that my joy may be in you and that your joy may be complete' (John 15:10, 11).

STUDY 2
GOD'S EVERLASTING COVENANT

QUESTIONS

DAY 1 *1 Chronicles 16:17-22; Genesis 17:1-7.*
a) What was the full title for the ark (15:25-26)?
b) What was central to all the wonderful acts of the Lord to Israel in the past (16:15-17)?

DAY 2 *1 Chronicles 16:23-36, 43.*
a) What attributes of God does David exalt in this magnificent song of praise?
b) Spend time praising the Lord, by reading these verses again.

DAY 3 *1 Chronicles 17:1-15.*
a) What had David in mind when he wanted to build a house for the Lord?
b) What did God mean when He said He would build a house for David (v. 10)?

DAY 4 *1 Chronicles 17:16-27*
a) What glimpses do you get of David's character from this prayer?
b) What things does David acknowledge will last for ever (vv. 22-24, 27)?

DAY 5 *1 Chronicles 18:1-6, 13-14.*
a) How was God keeping His everlasting covenant (vv. 6, 13-14)?
b) Chapter 19 gives an account of the battle with the Ammonites. What was the slogan of David's army in verse 13 of this chapter?

DAY 6 *1 Chronicles 18:7-11; 20:1-2.*
a) What treasures did David collect from his enemies?
b) What did he do with them?

DAY 7 *1 Chronicles 21:18–22:1; 2 Chronicles 3:1.*
Think over verse 24.
a) What could it mean for you?
b) Why did the threshing floor of Araunah become significant?

NOTES

Dear Hodaviah and Akkub,
As you hear this part of the Chronicler's sermon, are you beginning to see how the history of long ago is relevant to you? True, the ark of the covenant of the Lord was destroyed some 200 years before your time, but don't you see now that it was not the ark itself, but the COVENANT, which was important? It was not the box symbolizing God's presence which was worshipped even in David's day, it was the Lord God Himself. David's psalm of praise makes this quite clear. You – and we – can still praise the Lord in the words of this psalm, for He is still the same today. God's covenant is everlasting, and you, dear friends, are links in the chain. As you remain true to Him, you are part of that 'house' that the Lord promised to build, of David's line.

And did you notice David's reaction to the fact that God had not chosen him to build the temple, but his son? Sometimes we have to accept the fact that the work which we would dearly like to do for the Lord, is not in fact the one which He has for us. Let's learn a lesson from David about humility, and rejoice when others get the honour we have coveted.

But we can still imagine your longing for a king like David, who would fight battles and win fame and wealth. You are impressed by this account of David's power and greatness. But was it David's power? Was it David's greatness? I think you will agree that it was the Lord God who gave the victories, the Lord God who had the power, and the Lord God who was the truly great Ruler of His people.

One of the early Christians, long after your time, said that God's power is 'made perfect in weakness'. Take heart, my friends! The Lord simply requires of you what He required of David: that you do what is just and right for other people, and look to Him for victory.

And if you could peer into our century, you would not see the king of God's people on a throne like David was, for our King is invisible. But our invisible King is more powerful than David ever was. He is greater by far, His fame has spread more widely than David's, and His wealth is unlimited!

One day we will meet you around His throne, along with David and millions of others who have served Him through the ages, and together we will say with a loud voice –

'The kingdom of the world has become the kingdom of our Lord and of his Christ and he will reign for ever and ever' (Rev. 11:15).

Till then, we remain,
Your brothers and sisters in the Lord.

(A covenant is a promise or undertaking by one person to another to do something for that person. The promise may be accepted or rejected but never changed. In the covenant God promises certain things to different people notably Abraham (and later David) and his descendants. It also applies to the covenant with Israel at Mount Sinai.)

STUDY 3
THE KINGDOM OF GOD

QUESTIONS

DAY 1   *1 Chronicles 22:2-5, 17-19.*
a) In what ways did David prepare for the building of the temple?
b) How can this principle of devotion for the Lord's kingdom work out for us today (2 Cor. 8:1-5, 12)?

DAY 2   *1 Chronicles 22:6-16.*
a) What was the promise that God gave to David for Solomon?
b) What was David's wish for his son?
c) How did he encourage him?

DAY 3   *1 Chronicles 28:1-10 (compare v. 5 with 22:10).*
a) Whose kingdom was Solomon to rule over?
b) Why was Solomon told that his devotion must be wholehearted, and not a pretence (see also Prov. 16:2)?

DAY 4   *1 Chronicles 28:11-21.*
a) How did Solomon get to know the plans for the temple?
b) Who gave Moses plans for the tabernacle (Exod. 25:1, 2, 8, 9)?
c) Matthew 16:18. Do you think the Lord Jesus has a plan to be followed in the building of His church?

DAY 5   *1 Chronicles 29:1-9; 2 Corinthians 9:6.*
a) What challenge did David give the whole assembly?
b) What was the result?
c) What challenge is given to us in the New Testament reading?

DAY 6   *1 Chronicles 29:10.*
a) List the attributes of the Lord in David's prayer (vv. 10-13).
b) Whose is the kingdom?
c) Take a few minutes to meditate carefully on verses 14-18. What can you identify with in these verses?

DAY 7   *1 Chronicles 29:21-30.*
a) How is the throne described in verse 23?
b) David's prayer for Solomon at this time is recorded in Psalm 72. Look especially at verses 1, 5, 8 and 17. From our viewpoint in this century, who is the 'royal son' who sits on the throne?

NOTES

Do you believe God has a plan for your life? Do you believe He has chosen you for a particular work in His Kingdom and in the building of His Church?

Scripture confirms that 'God gives ability to everyone for their particular service' (I Cor. 12:6 GNB).

CHOSEN
David said: 'The Lord *chose* Judah as leader; He *chose* my family; He *chose* me to be king over Israel; He has *chosen* my son Solomon to sit on the throne; Solomon, the Lord has *chosen* you to build'.

Peter wrote that Jesus Christ was the chosen and precious cornerstone. He said that the people were 'a *chosen* people' and 'living stones ... being built into a spiritual house' (I Pet. 2:4, 9).

THE PLANS
How can you know what God's plans are for you, for your church, for the advance of His kingdom today?

Well, how did David know?

David gave Solomon 'the plans of all that the Spirit had put in his mind' (28:12).

The Lord gave David 'understanding in all the details of the plan' (v. 19).

Will the Lord do any less today for those who serve Him with wholehearted devotion and with a willing mind, who are willing to consecrate themselves to the Lord?

The Lord says, 'I know the plans I have for you' (Jer. 29:11).

THE KINGDOM
The people of the Chronicler's day might have bemoaned the fact that the throne of the kingdom of Israel was no more. They could not see a king in all the glory of David or Solomon, so the Chronicler makes it clear that Solomon was to sit on 'the throne of the kingdom of the Lord', which is an everlasting kingdom.

'Take heart,' he says to his contemporaries, 'that earthly kingdom was but a picture of the real thing. The real kingdom is God's kingdom, and He is head over all'.

David said to God: 'Yours, O Lord is the kingdom ... you are the ruler of all things' (29:11, 12). He is just as truly King in our day as He was in David's.

Today there are people belonging to God's kingdom in almost every country of the world. Let us remember that we serve, not an earthly, but a heavenly king, Jesus, about whom it is written: 'Your throne, O God, will last for ever and ever, and righteousness will be the sceptre of your kingdom' (Heb. 1:8).

The Lord's Prayer, as Jesus gave it in Matthew 6:9-13, ends with the words 'deliver us from the evil one'. Read I Chronicles 29:11 again, and see how the familiar ending to the Lord's Prayer has been drawn from this verse.

Say the Lord's Prayer together as a group.

STUDY 4
WORSHIP
QUESTIONS

DAY 1 2 Chronicles 1:1-6; Hebrews 10:25.
a) Where did Solomon go?
b) Why did he go there?
c) Who went with him?
d) What did he take with him?

DAY 2 2 Chronicles 1:7-13.
a) Try to picture this scene. How does it contrast with the one we read about yesterday?
b) What was Solomon's deepest desire?
c) What should ours be (Eph. 1:17; Jas. 1:5)?

DAY 3 2 Chronicles 2:1-10.
a) Why did Solomon want the very best materials and workmen when building the temple?
b) In what areas of our lives can we give God the best we have? (Some suggestions to start you thinking: John 4:24; Eph. 1:4; 2 Cor. 9:7; 2 Tim. 2:15.)

DAY 4 2 Chronicles 2:11-3:2.
a) What did King Hiram, who was not an Israelite, say about God?
b) Why do you think he acknowledged these things (Matt. 5:16)?

DAY 5 2 Chronicles 5:1-10.
a) What was the significance of bringing the ark to the temple?
b) What was inside the ark (Heb. 9:4-5)?

DAY 6 2 Chronicles 5:11-14; 1 Corinthians 3:16.
a) What was the purpose of the music that was played and sung?
b) What happened next?
c) What do you think this meant?

DAY 7 2 Chronicles 6:1-11; John 16:7, 13; Romans 8:26-27.
a) It has been suggested that David, as a man of victory, was a type of Jesus, the Son of God. Referring to the New Testament verses, in what ways was Solomon a type of the Holy Spirit at this stage?
b) What does Solomon say about the THRONE and the TEMPLE in verse 10?

NOTES

What aspects of worship have we discovered in this study?

1. Worship is a conscious act. Like Solomon, we must seek out the Lord, and come deliberately into His presence with a desire to worship Him.

2. Worship can be a corporate act. A 'togetherness' in worship is uplifting to those involved, and Hebrews 10:25 urges us to encourage one another in this way.

3. True worship involves consecration. Solomon brought a costly offering to the Lord, which, in the tradition of the Israelite faith, signified the consecration to God of the offerer's own heart. The New Testament equivalent is stated in Romans 12:1, 'offer your bodies as living sacrifices, holy and pleasing to God'.

4. Worship is intimate communion between God and the worshipper. Our Heavenly Father wants us to be alone with Him, and to spend time worshipping Him. Do you meet with Him each day, to read His word and talk to Him as a child talks to his father?
   Madame Guyon, a seventeenth century French mystic who was imprisoned – simply for the 'crime' of loving God with a degree of spirituality few have attained, wrote this:

   'Why do we come to the Lord? Do you come to Him for sweetness? Do you come to Him because it is enjoyable to be in the Lord's presence? Let me recommend a higher way.
   As you come to the Lord to pray, bring a full heart of pure love that is not seeking anything for itself. Bring a heart that is seeking nothing from the Lord, but desire only to please Him, to do His will. So, dear Christian, do not come to prayer for spiritual enjoyment. Do not even come to experience your Lord.
   Then what? Come ... just to please Him.'

5. Worship is giving God the best we have to offer. Remember our Lord's words to the Samaritan woman that worshippers must worship in 'spirit and in truth' (John 4:24). This means giving God the best, in all areas of our lives.

6. Our worship brings glory to God.
   As we become true worshippers, the effects may surprise us. Friends who are not Christians may, like Hiram King of Tyre, recognize the Lord in our lives as 'the fragrance of the knowledge of him' spreads everywhere through us (2 Cor. 2:14).

7. Worship helps us to remember what God is like, and to acknowledge what He has done for us. You might like to use some of the Psalms (e.g. 8, 23, 33, 89) as you worship the Lord in your own quiet time.

8. Music is a divine gift for use in worship.

Throughout the Bible we see music as a prominent part of worship:
- the songs of Moses and Miriam (Exod. 15)
- the psalms of David (Ps. 95:1; 104:33; 150)
- the words of the apostle Paul (Eph. 5:19; Col. 3:16)
- the great music of heaven as described in Revelation.

Today, Christian music is available to us at the flick of a switch. In your time alone with God, why not try worshipping Him with your cassette or CD player?

With today's study fresh in our minds, let us determine to give worship a more central place in our lives. It should not be confined to Sundays, in church! Remember that we like 'living stones are being built into a spiritual house' (1 Pet. 2:5), and that our bodies are temples of the Holy Spirit. A temple is essentially a place of worship at all times.

STUDY 5
WORSHIP – THE LORD'S RESPONSE

QUESTIONS

DAY 1 *2 Chronicles 6:12-21; Hebrews 11:6; Nehemiah 1:5; Daniel 9:4.*
a) Faith in who God is, should come first in prayer. How does Solomon describe God in these verses?
b) How would you, today, answer the question in verse 18 (see John 1:14)?

DAY 2 *2 Chronicles 6:22-40; Nehemiah 1:6.*
a) Solomon is concerned for his people. List seven situations which he feels may occur and for which they will need God's help.
b) What must happen before God can 'hear and forgive'?

DAY 3 *2 Chronicles 6:41–7:10; Leviticus 9:23-24; 1 Kings 18:37-39.*
a) What was the Lord's response to Solomon's prayer (look carefully at 2 Chron. 7:3 again)?
b) How do you think the people felt about God? And how did they feel after the festival was over?

DAY 4 *2 Chronicles 7:11-22.*
a) What response did the Lord give to Solomon in private, in answer to his requests? (Note the condition – 'if'.)
b) What would happen if the people did no fulfil the condition?

DAY 5 *2 Chronicles 8:12-18.*
a) What things was Solomon careful to do, as laid down by Moses and also by his father David?
b) What did Jesus say we must be careful to do (John 15:9-15)?

DAY 6 *2 Chronicles 9:1-12; 2 Chronicles 1:10.*
a) Why did the Queen of Sheba come to Jerusalem?
b) What was her reaction to Solomon's wisdom?
c) What did she say about Solomon's God? (Compare this with 2 Chron. 2:11.)

DAY 7 *2 Chronicles 9:17-31.*
a) What impression do you get of Solomon from these verses?
b) What did all his wealth mean for the people (v. 27)?
c) What parallel do you see with this in Colossians 2:2-3?

NOTES

The Chronicler, in this part of his sermon, shows very clearly that God is concerned for his people. As God is eternally the same, it is an encouragement for God's people of every age to know that He is willing to listen and respond to them.

SOLOMON'S PRAYER
Solomon prayed that there would be a response from God when the people sinned, when there was no rain, when there was famine, etc. If he had not expected a response, there would have been no point in interceding for his people in this way. This was no mere ritual, or meaningless words spoken to impress. This was an earnest entreaty, a prayer which pleaded for an answer, and that answer was vital to his people's future.

Are your prayers like this? Do you intercede for others with the same earnestness? And do you expect God to answer?

GOD'S RESPONSE
Solomon may not have expected such a dramatic answer to his prayer. How gracious our Lord is! By His divine action He sent fire, which everyone could see, to consume the sacrifices and thus accept their gifts. This must have reminded the people in Solomon's day of the time when Moses witnessed a similar event And the people of the Chronicler's day would also have remembered the story of Elijah on Mt. Carmel (I Kgs. 18:37-39). The Lord again showed the people His glory, and we can only imagine what a wonderful sight that must have been.

THE MEANING
What did this part of the sermon mean for people living in the fourth century BC? They also had a focal point for their worship, the temple built after the return from exile. But notice that it is not in the temple, however, where God dwells. The highest heavens cannot contain Him. The condition He sets out in order that He will hear and forgive them, is that they repent and turn to Him. There WILL be a response, even if they don't see fire coming down, or experience His glory in any other visible way.

What does it mean for us? 'Will God really dwell on the earth with men?' The answer is 'YES' – a glorious YES! He has! Jesus has come to demonstrate how willingly God hears our prayers, and to shed His blood so that God can forgive when sinners turn to Him and confess their sin. And God's Son came to show that there will be a response from God the Father to our prayers.

We learned last week that to worship is:

1) To come consciously into His presence, either alone or with others,
2) To recognize that our worship pleases the Father and brings glory to Him,
3) To acknowledge and remind ourselves of what God is like,
4) To offer ourselves to God.

We can now add another point:

5) True worship involves expecting to hear a response from Him.

Think carefully about your own private worship this week. Maybe you can develop a two-way communication with your Heavenly Father if, after you have followed the first four points above, you wait in quietness before Him, expecting a response. You may experience His peace in a new way, or 'see' His smile, feel His arms around you, or hear Him speak through some verses in His word. Wait for it. Don't give up!

'True worshippers will worship the Father in spirit and in truth, for they are the kind of worshippers the Father seeks' (John 4:23).

STUDY 6

THE KINGDOM DIVIDED

QUESTIONS

DAY 1 *2 Chronicles 9:30–10:5.*
a) Who was Rehoboam's father? Who was his grandfather?
b) What can you find out about Jeroboam from 1 Kings 11:26-40?

DAY 2 *2 Chronicles 10:6.*
a) Rehoboam had a choice. What did he decide to do?
b) Discuss verse 15. Do you think Rehoboam was responsible before God for his actions?

DAY 3 *2 Chronicles 11:1-4, 13-17; 1 Kings 12:26.*
a) What did the Lord forbid Rehoboam to do?
b) How are we shown that the southern kingdom (Rehoboam's) was initially strong spiritually?

DAY 4 *2 Chronicles 12:1-12, 16; 1 Kings 14:21-24.*
a) Why did the Lord allow the king of Egypt to attack?
b) What good thing did the leaders and the king do?
c) What was the result?

DAY 5 *2 Chronicles 13:1-9.*
a) Abijah accuses Jeroboam and his people of three ways in which they have sinned against the Lord. What are they?
b) Luke 1:30-33. What did the angel tell Mary about the throne and the kingdom?

DAY 6 *2 Chronicles 13:9; Acts 5:38-39.*
a) What did Abijah claim for himself and his people?
b) Which verse links the 'Chronicles' reading and the 'Acts' reading?
c) Romans 8:31. Do you believe this?

DAY 7 *2 Chronicles 13:3, 13.*
a) Humanly speaking, which side should have won this battle?
b) What actually happened?

NOTES

The Chronicler has written at length about David's THRONE and Solomon's TEMPLE.
Now the glorious days of David and Solomon are over. The kingdom is divided, never to be reunited.
Don't be put off by the strange sounding names of the kings in the studies from this point on. They are the names of real people, so learn how to pronounce them until they become familiar.

REHOBOAM	JEROBOAM
Solomon's son	In trouble with Solomon
David's grandson	No royal pedigree
Married to Absalom's daughter	A hard worker
Sincere worshippers sided with him	Drove out the priests
The Temple was in his kingdom	Made idols and set up shrines

One might think that Rehoboam couldn't go wrong. But in spite of all his God-given advantages, Rehoboam was a failure in God's sight.

So, says the Chronicler, David's throne and Solomon's temple do not guarantee a right relationship with God. They possess no magical, automatic powers, they have no virtue in themselves. God looks on the heart, and, in spite of a few glimmers of humility during his reign, Rehoboam 'did evil because he had not set his heart on seeking the Lord' (12:14).

ABIJAH

Son of Rehoboam, he became king over Judah, the southern kingdom. Although the older historical book of Kings dismisses Abijah as one who 'committed all the sins his father had done before him' (I Kgs. 15:3), the Chronicler records a most interesting speech by him to the people of the north. It shows that then, at least, Abijah had a very real grasp of the spiritual principles which the Chronicler himself wished to convey.

Abijah stated that:

– The kingship of Israel belongs to the Lord.
– He has delegated it to the house of David.
– In Rehoboam, the system went wrong.
– But now, the kingdom of the Lord is again in the hands of a truly Davidic king (himself).
– The southern kingdom is on the Lord's side.

From this point on, the Chronicler concentrates on Judah, the southern kingdom, which, he maintains, is the true Israel. (We may find it confusing that he sometimes uses the term 'Israel' for the north, and sometimes for the south!)

ONE LORD JESUS CHRIST

How beautifully He fulfils the promise: 'the Lord, the God of Israel, has given the kingship of Israel to David and his descendants for ever' (2 Chron. 13:5).

The angel Gabriel said: 'The Lord God will give Him the throne of His father David, and he will reign over the house of Jacob for ever: his kingdom will never end' (Luke 1:32-33).

Can you see how the purposes of God run right through the Old and New Testaments, up to our day – and beyond? The Jewish kingdom was divided in Rehoboam's day, but Christ came to break down barriers, and to reconcile in one body all those who put their trust in Him, irrespective of race, colour or background. Our allegiance is to the King of the Kingdom which will never end!

STUDY 7
A LESSON IN TRUSTING GOD

QUESTIONS

DAY 1 *2 Chronicles 14:1-7.*
a) What is recorded about Asa in verse 2?
b) Could the same be said about you?
c) How is God described in verses 2, 4 and 7?

DAY 2 *2 Chronicles 14:8-15.*
a) How was Asa's faith put to the test?
b) Read aloud Asa's prayer in verse 11, in as many versions as possible.
c) Can you think of any situation in your own life where you might want to use the thoughts conveyed in this prayer?

DAY 3 *2 Chronicles 15:1-7.*
a) How do we know that Azariah was giving Asa God's message?
b) What is the promise contained in all the following references: Deuteronomy 4:29; 1 Chronicles 28:9; Jeremiah 29:13 and Matthew 7:7?
c) Which verse in today's reading also contains this promise? What does it mean to you?

DAY 4 *2 Chronicles 15:8-15.*
a) What additional people had settled in the southern kingdom?
b) Why had they come?
c) How had the people proved the truth of verse 2?

DAY 5 *2 Chronicles 15:16-19; 11:20-22.*
a) What further religious reform did Asa carry out?
b) Read in several versions what is said about Asa in verse 17 and write down the one that impresses you most? Do you know anyone like that?

DAY 6 *2 Chronicles 16:1-6 (Living Bible is helpful).*
To understand this passage, try to find a map to show where Ramah was, and also the country of Aram (Syria). What did Asa do that doesn't seem in keeping with what we read yesterday?

DAY 7 *2 Chronicles 16:7-14.*
a) What did God, through His prophet, accuse Asa of doing, and not doing?
b) Write verse 9 in your own words, to share with your group.

NOTES

What does the Chronicler want to illustrate by the reign of King Asa? Asa was a good-hearted, God-fearing person though very human and far from perfect. But a clear lesson emerges from the facts given about him, and the central thought in this section is that spoken by Azariah the prophet and inspired by the Holy Spirit: 'The Lord is with you when you are with him. If you seek him, he will be found by you, but if you forsake him, he will forsake you' (15:2).

Let's see how this proved correct in Asa's life.

1) Although he did not inherit godly ways from his father or his grandfather, nor did his grandmother guide him along the right track, his desire when he came to the throne was to do what was good and right in the eyes of the Lord.

Consequence: No war during those years, for the Lord gave him rest.

2) When an enemy did march against him, Asa relied totally on the Lord.

Consequence: The Lord fought the battle for him, and gave Asa and his army an overwhelming victory.

3) After hearing the prophet's message, Asa undertook further reforms, and called his people to rededicate themselves to the Lord.

Consequence: All Judah rejoiced and sought God eagerly, and the Lord gave them rest on every side.

4) He made a treaty with the King of Syria (Aram), paying him with the gold and silver from the temple.

Consequence: A severe rebuke from the Lord through His prophet, and a challenge – he could have defeated the Syrians if he had relied on the Lord.

5) The last picture we have of Asa is interesting. The seer rebukes him for failing to rely on the Lord. Asa is angry; he puts the seer in prison and brutally oppresses some of his people. Asa has a severe disease of the feet; he does not seek help from the Lord and dies.

However, the people give him a magnificent funeral, acknowledging that for most of his life he has been a great king.

Although Asa was king on the THRONE, although he had the TEMPLE with its ritual and its treasures, these did not prevent him from going his own way and choosing not to rely on the Lord when it suited him.

Surely it was clear to the people of the Chronicler's day, that the eyes of the Lord were still ranging throughout the earth, looking for those whose hearts were fully committed to Him.

And God is the same today.

Do you feel challenged by this study?
Have you sought and found the Lord yet?

If so, are you fully committed to Him, so that nothing can distract you from relying on Him?

We can praise the Lord because, as Christians, we not only have the desire to do what is right in the eyes of the Lord, but we also have the power to overcome temptation and to live a godly life, because His Spirit lives within us.

Perhaps you have sung this hymn, which takes its thought from chapter 14:11 (AV), in the days when Asa's faith shone brightly:

> We rest on Thee, our Shield and our Defender,
> We go not forth alone against the foe,
> Strong in Thy strength, safe in Thy keeping tender,
> We rest on Thee, and in Thy name we go.'

STUDY 8

WEAKNESS AND STRENGTH

QUESTIONS

DAY 1   *2 Chronicles 17:1-13.*
a) What are we told about Jehoshaphat's relationship with God (vv. 3, 4, 6)?
b) What was his military strategy (vv. 2, 12, 13)?

DAY 2   *2 Chronicles 18:1-27; 1 Kings 16:30; 21:25-26.*
a) What do we know about Ahab, king of the northern kingdom?
b) Can you find three things Jehoshaphat should not have done (vv. 1-3)?

DAY 3   *2 Chronicles 18:28–19:3.*
a) Discuss what part God played in this battle.
b) What did God, through His prophet, rebuke Jehoshaphat for?

DAY 4   *2 Chronicles 19:4-11.*
a) How did Jehoshaphat show his people that he was personally concerned for their welfare?
b) What did he instruct the judges to do?

DAY 5   *2 Chronicles 20:1-13; 6:28-30.*
a) What was Jehoshaphat's first reaction when he heard of the advancing army?
b) What did the people do when they heard?
c) How did he describe to God the way they felt?

DAY 6   *2 Chronicles 20:14-19.*
a) What surprising message did Jahaziel deliver from the Lord?
b) How did Jehoshaphat and all the people respond?

DAY 7   *2 Chronicles 20:20-30.*
a) What preparations did Jehoshaphat make for the battle?
b) What did everyone do after they had carried off the plunder from the enemy?
(You may like to read on to the end of Chapter 20.)

NOTES

Isn't the Bible graphic in description? Can't you just see the events happening in this fascinating chapter? Jehoshaphat is the central figure, so let's consider him as the God-appointed shepherd of his people and then look at his weakness, and finally his strength.

Jehoshaphat – shepherd of his people
We have seen how caring Jehoshaphat was, how concerned for righteousness and justice for his people, and how he educated them in the ways of the Lord. What a splendid example! He is likened to King David, who was a man after God's own heart. His character is moulded by his personal devotion to the Lord. Notice chapter 17 verse 4: 'He obeyed the commandments of his father's God – quite unlike the people across the border in the land of Israel' (LB).

Jehoshaphat – his weakness
It was probably his very nature, the fact that he was kind and considerate, that made it hard for him to say 'no'. This seems to have been his weakness. It led him into trouble and almost cost him his life.

Step 1.   He did not have to ally himself with Ahab, the wicked king of Israel, by marriage. He already had great wealth and honour, and he had God.

Step 2.   He did not need to make a state visit to Ahab – though because of Step 1 perhaps it was a natural thing to do.

Step 3.   He should not have agreed to fight alongside Ahab. He made a feeble attempt to stick to his principles by asking Ahab to seek counsel from the Lord: But it was obvious that Ahab was in command and wanted things his way

Step 4.   A narrow escape and a rebuke from the Lord.

Is there not a lesson here for us as Christians? If we cannot say 'no' to what is wrong at Step 1, we shall be drawn into further steps away from God's plan for us. If you are in any kind of wrong relationship as you read these notes, come honestly before the Lord and ask him to make you strong to break with what is not pleasing to Him.

Jehoshaphat – his strength
Although he did not recognize the weakness in his character, he was certainly aware of his country's weakness in the face of the vast army that was approaching.

So, what did he do? He immediately sought the Lord, and called his people to do the same.

In World War II, Britain's leaders called the people to a National Day of Prayer when the troops were trapped in France with no way of escape from the advancing army. The Lord caused low clouds to lie over the sea between Dunkirk and Dover, and thousands of small craft were able to rescue the troops without fear of attack from enemy planes overhead.

Our God is the same yesterday, today and for ever. It is thrilling to read how HE fought the battle for His people in Jehoshaphat's day as they lifted their hearts and voices in praise to Him.

The Lord could surely have said to Jehoshaphat, as he did to Paul: 'my power is strongest when you are weak' (2 Cor. 12:9 GNB), and Jehoshaphat could have realized, as Paul did, that when he was weak, he was strong!

STUDY 9
DIVINE JUSTICE – GOD IS NOT MOCKED

QUESTIONS

Don't let these names put you off. Remember they were men who were as real as you are!

DAY 1 JEHORAM: *2 Chronicles 21:1-7, 12-20.*
a) Why did God not destroy the kingdom of Judah completely?
b) How was the prophecy from Elijah fulfilled?

DAY 2 AHAZIAH: *2 Chronicles 22:1-4, 8-12; 1 Kings 21:25.*
a) How was Ahaziah influenced when he became king?
b) How did Athaliah try to make sure she would be queen and in full control?
c) How did the Lord overrule?

DAY 3 JOASH: *2 Chronicles 23:1-3, 11-17, 21.*
a) Six years later, what did the priest Jehoiada do?
b) Compare verses 3, 11 and 16 with 24:15-16. What can be said about Jehoiada?
c) How did divine justice catch up with Athaliah?

DAY 4 *2 Chronicles 24:1-13.*
a) What new idea did Joash have for collecting money to repair the temple?
b) How did the people give?

DAY 5 *2 Chronicles 24:17-25; Luke 11:50-51.*
a) When Joash and the people had forsaken God, what happened?
b) After Joash had plotted against Zechariah the priest and killed him, what did his officials do (v. 25)?

DAY 6 AMAZIAH and UZZIAH: *2 Chronicles 25:1, 2, 27; 26:1-5, 16-21.*
a) In what ways were Uzziah and his father Amaziah alike?
b) Read Isaiah 6:1. After Uzziah's fifty-two year-long reign, how did God show the prophet Isaiah that He was still in control?

DAY 7 JOTHAM: *2 Chronicles 27:1-9.*
a) What good things do we read about Jotham and what happened as a consequence?
b) Who was the last king before Jotham to die peacefully? (Don't look up 2 Chron. 21:1 until you have thought about it!)
c) Compare how these two kings died with the way the five kings in between met their deaths.

NOTES

Were these really the 'good old days' that the people of the Chronicler's day looked back to? This was surely the time when the kingdom of Judah was at its lowest ebb, and heading for disaster.

BUT GOD ...
'Nevertheless, because of the covenant the Lord had made with David, the Lord was not willing to destroy the house of David' (21:7). What a long-suffering God we have!

JEHOSHAPHAT: (Study 8) did what was right in the eyes of the Lord.
Reigned twenty-five years.
JEHORAM: First born son, married Athaliah, daughter of the infamous Ahab and Jezebel. He led Judah away from the Lord.
Reigned eight years.
AHAZIAH: The only son left. Did evil in the eyes of the Lord. He was murdered while visiting Ahab's son.
Reigned one year.
ATHALIAH: Mother of Ahaziah. Seized power, killed all her grandsons except one.
Reigned six years.

In less than fifteen years, through influence of evil men and the pagan idolatress Athaliah, the kingdom of Judah was brought to the brink of ruin.

* * *

BUT GOD ...
God had promised David that He would establish his throne for ever – that is, that He would preserve the descendants of David till the One came who would rule for ever.
But Jehoram killed all his brothers,
The Philistines took away all his sons – except one,
Athaliah murdered all those in line to the throne – except one.

Can't you see how God was faithfully keeping His covenant?
What more colourful storybook character is there than the Wicked Queen? And here is one in real life. The account is dramatic:

The Wicked Queen orders full-scale slaughter of the whole royal family, but the aunt of baby Joash secretly rescues him and hides him in a room. As soon as she can, she transfers him to the temple where she and her husband the priest live.
The baby grows into a little boy and still has to be kept hidden. Plans are made. The priest works quietly. Secretly, leaders of the people are summoned to Jerusalem.
'The King's son shall reign, as the Lord promised.'
The day has come. The people are gathered, and the priest brings out seven year old Joash and crowns him king. What shouting and rejoicing!

The Wicked Queen hears the noise and rushes out. She catches sight of the little boy king, wearing the crown and royal robes. Who can this be? Has she not killed all those who might have a claim to the throne?

'Treason,' she screams.

But no one comes to her aid. Instead, some of the priest's men seize her and put her to an ignominious death.

* * *

The next four kings are a mixture of good and bad:

JOASH:	A good beginning, a bad ending. Reigned forty years.
AMAZIAH:	Turned away from following the Lord. Reigned twenty-nine years.
UZZIAH:	After he became powerful, his pride led to his downfall. Reigned fifty-two years.
JOTHAM:	Recognised that his power depended on obedience to the Lord. Reigned sixteen years.

BUT GOD brings His divine justice to bear on each one.

STUDY 10
RESTORING RELATIONSHIPS

QUESTIONS

DAY 1 *2 Chronicles 28:1, 5-15, 27.*
a) What made the Lord so very angry with the men of Israel (the northern kingdom).
b) What similarities can you find between verses 14 and 15 and the story Jesus told in Luke 10:30-35?

DAY 2 *2 Chronicles 29:1-11, 15-17; Luke 19:45-46.*
a) How did Hezekiah immediately set about restoring the relationship between the people and God?
b) What had the priests and Levites to do?

DAY 3 *2 Chronicles 29:25; 1 Chronicles 15:16; 16:7-8.*
a) What were the two main features of the service of the temple?
b) What was the reason for the great rejoicing (v. 36)?

DAY 4 *2 Chronicles 30:1-9; 2 Kings 18:9-12.*
a) What did Hezekiah do that had not been done since the kingdom was divided?
b) From the reading in 2 Kings find out what happened to the people in the northern kingdom (Israel). This will explain what Hezekiah wrote in his letter (v. 6).

DAY 5 *2 Chronicles 30:10, 26, 27.*
a) What reactions did the couriers encounter?
b) When the people who had gathered in Jerusalem obeyed the Lord's commands as given to Moses, what was the result?

DAY 6 *2 Chronicles 31:1-10, 20, 21.*
a) What further evidence was there that God had blessed His people?
b) How does this chapter illustrate 2 Corinthians 9:7?

DAY 7 *2 Chronicles 32:1, 6, 16-26. (Read the whole story as you prepare at home.)*
a) How did Hezekiah encourage his military officers?
b) After receiving Sennacherib's letters, what did Hezekiah do? (See also 2 Kgs. 19:14.)

NOTES

1. *With those who are enemies.*
What an amazing account we have in chapter 28 about the soldiers caring for their prisoners and escorting them back home!
   When the Lord Jesus wanted to teach people to love their neighbours whoever they were, he told the parable of the Good Samaritan. Isn't it likely that, knowing the Old Testament as He did, He had this incident in mind when He thought up the story?

The Lord is still concerned that His people should break down all barriers and show love to everyone, without discrimination. How do you measure up?

2. *With God.*
Hezekiah realized that the only way he and his people could cope with the future, was to look first to God. To restore this relationship meant giving God His proper place, in this case, re-establishing the temple services as in the 'golden age' of the nation. Notice how this involved worship and sacrifice.

So today, to live in a right relationship with God, we need to worship Him personally 'in spirit and in truth' (John 4:24), and to offer our bodies as 'living sacrifices, holy and pleasing to God' (Rom. 12:1).

3. *With fellow believers.*
   The kingdom had been divided, with both sides antagonistic to one another since the days of Solomon's son, some 200 years before. The Assyrian invasion of Israel in the sixth year of Hezekiah's reign, devastated that country. It was never to be the same again. Now Hezekiah sends out an offer of friendship, of reconciliation. They all worship the one true God. Can't they bury their differences and unite in the celebration of the Passover?

Sadly, in our world today, there are bitter divisions among Christians – even in the same town. It is not Hezekiah, but the Lord Jesus, who begs us to come to 'complete unity to let the world know that you (God) sent me' (John 17:23).

4. *No relationship with Satan.*
   Sennacherib here typifies Satan, as he scorns and ridicules the Lord God, tries to get God's people to doubt His power, and speaks about Him as if He were just one of the many idols of that day.
   Hezekiah's confidence in God was strong, and he took this crisis to the Lord in prayer. Like Jehoshaphat before him he knew that only God could save him from the enemy. And God showed His mighty power!

We read the same message in the New Testament from the pen of the apostle John: '... every spirit that does not acknowledge Jesus is not from God. This is the spirit of the antichrist ...

You, dear children, are from God and have overcome them, because the one who is in you is greater than the one who is in the world' (I John 4:3-4).

* * *

With Hezekiah's reign, the Chronicler is once more able to highlight his theme of the **THRONE** and the **TEMPLE**.

The **THRONE**, because here is a king who comes nearest to the ideal that God has for a king, since David.

The **TEMPLE**, because not only are repairs made (as in Joash's day), but the whole system of worship and sacrifice is celebrated in a way that has not been seen since the days of Solomon.

STUDY 11
GOD WORKS OUT HIS PURPOSES

QUESTIONS

DAY 1 *2 Chronicles 33:1-13, 21-23.*
a) What does Manasseh's story teach us about God?
b) How was Amon like his father, and how did he differ from him?

DAY 2 *2 Chronicles 34:1-3, 8-13.*
a) What did Josiah do, that had not been done since the days of his forefather Hezekiah?
b) Where did the money come from for this project?

DAY 3 *2 Chronicles 34:14-21; Deuteronomy 12:1-6; 17:18-19.*
a) Why was Josiah so distressed, in these verses?
b) Find two of the commands which were written in the Book of the Law of the Lord.

DAY 4 *2 Chronicles 34:22-33.*
a) Why did God, through the prophetess Huldah, commend Josiah?
b) After reading the Book to all the people, what did the king do?

DAY 5 *2 Chronicles 35:1-6, 16-19; 2 Kings 23:25.*
a) Why do you think it was important to go back to what David, Solomon and Moses had written?
b) Where should we go back to in our worship of God?

DAY 6 *2 Chronicles 36:1-14.*
a) What happened to Jehoahaz? Jehoiakim (see also Jer. 22:18-19)? Jehoiachin?
b) How would you describe the reign of Zedekiah?

DAY 7 *2 Chronicles 36:15-23; Jeremiah 25:8-11.*
a) Summarize verses 15-19 as if God was speaking.
b) How did God give the nation of Israel hope?

NOTES

Dear brothers and sisters in the Lord,

Hodaviah and I wish to thank you for your concern for us and our people. We have seen quite clearly now from the Chronicler's sermon that divine justice cannot fail – sin will be punished. We have also seen that divine grace cannot fail either – good and bad kings there have been, but God has kept His covenant promise, and by His grace He gave the crown to David's descendants for ever.

Wasn't the story of Manasseh interesting? Especially interesting to us, as it is a picture of what actually happened later to our nation. Because of sin, God brought punishment in the form of the kings of Babylon, who carried the people off captive, just as they did with Manasseh. However, we are encouraged today because God brought our nation back to our land and resettled them after seventy years. We see that God forgives and renews His people when they truly humble themselves and turn to Him.

The Chronicler has made it clear that God was working out His purposes during those last days before the exile. Although Josiah made the people follow the ways of the Lord when he was alive, yet their hearts were far from Him, and after Josiah died, things went from bad to worse.

We do not grieve now that the throne and Solomon's temple are no more. They served the purpose for which God appointed them. When the right time came:

1. God dismantled the system. After the exile there would be a new era.
2. God deposed the leaders. Some kings and priests had done what they could, others violated God's law. God has promised that one day He will anoint ONE who will be a king and a priest for ever.
3. God punished the rebels. Retribution had to come to kings and people who were totally evil.
4. God established peace in His land. The ancient law of the sabbath rest for the land had been ignored, and now for seventy years it would make up for what it had missed.

So, my friends, we have hope. Hope in God as our King, and a sure hope that His eternal purposes will be fulfilled. We are a link in the chain of His dealings with mankind, as you are too. We know that one day a Redeemer will come, as the prophet Job predicted many years ago, that He will live for ever, and that because of Him, we shall see God.

Yours, rejoicing in that hope,
Akkub

ANSWER GUIDE

The following pages contain an Answer Guide. It is recommended that answers to the questions be attempted before turning to this guide. It is only a guide and the answers given should not be treated as exhaustive.

GUIDE TO INTRODUCTORY STUDY

To guide discussion on the three questions at the beginning, refer to Romans 15:4 and 2 Timothy 3:15-16. Think through your own views carefully beforehand.

An interest in family records is a characteristic of our times. People travel to the country of their origin, and take great pains to trace their ancestors as far back as they can go.

Finding one's roots gives a great sense of stability and continuity.

As you read through the dialogue, you will see that these people have, as we would say today, an identity crisis. The first nine chapters of I Chronicles show these people their roots. As Christian people today, we too need to go back to the roots of our faith, and understand that God is the same yesterday, today and forever.

The Divine principles in chapter 5:18-26 are found in verse 20 (Divine grace) and verses 25 and 26 (Divine justice).

* * *

(A group leader should prepare the following notes on Chapters 1–9 well. The notes need not be read to the group, but the facts conveyed in the leader's own manner.)

Think of the people of God throughout history as a Tree.

Chapters 1–3 The TRUNK of the Tree.

Glancing over chapter 1, which names are familiar? Underline them in your Bible.

Chapter 2 traces the genealogy from Israel (Jacob), through his son Judah, to David (2:15).

3:1-9 gives David's sons. How many were born to him in Hebron? How many while he reigned in Jerusalem? How many daughters are mentioned?

3:10-16 lists the succession of kings in JUDAH after David. We shall find out more about these kings later in our study.

3:17-24 gives the descendants of the royal line, even though there were no kings in this period after the exile.

3:24 is interesting, as these seven sons of Elioenai are the Chronicler's contemporaries. Can you spot the two in our dialogue?

Chapters 4–7 The BRANCHES of the Tree.
These chapters give the descendants of the twelve sons of Israel. Some interesting pictures emerge, showing glimpses of real, flesh-and-blood people, in the midst of all the bewildering names. Mark these verses in your Bible and make reference to them.

    4:9
    4:21, 23
    4:38-40
    5:1-2
    6:31-32
    7:21-23

Chapters 8–9 The FRUIT of the Tree – Kingship and Priesthood.
Chapter 8 traces the genealogy of Saul, the first KING.
Chapter 9 lists PRIESTS, Levites and temple servants.

    God is represented to His people by a king.
    They are represented to God by a priest.

This is at the centre of the Chronicles sermon, and consequently this study is entitled *The Throne and the Temple*.

GUIDE TO STUDY 1

DAY 1   a) He was unfaithful to the Lord. He did not keep the word of the Lord. He consulted a medium for guidance (1 Sam. 28:8) and did not enquire of the Lord.
                   b) Divine justice.

DAY 2   a) Shepherd and ruler (11:2).
                   b) The Lord Jesus; He is our Shepherd and King.
                   c) He was the one who led the military campaigns; he became more and more powerful; the Lord was with him.

DAY 3   a) He called all the people together to bring the ark to Jerusalem.
                   b) The king and people had not sought to find the will of God.

DAY 4   a) That He is holy, and that He requires obedience.
                   b) The Lord blessed Obed-Edom and his household.

DAY 5   a) The Lord established David as king and exalted his kingdom. He also gave him victory when he looked to the Lord for help.
b) To every land and nation.

DAY 6   a) The Levites were the only people allowed to carry the ark, and they were to carry it with the poles on their shoulders.
b) He blamed himself, as well as the people, for not enquiring of the Lord how to carry the ark in the proper way.

DAY 7   a) Seen: thousands of joyful people walking and dancing; the Levites carrying the ark.
   Heard: shouts of joy; the sound of rams' horns, cymbals, trumpets, the playing of lyres and harps.
b) They were to make petition, to give thanks, and to praise the Lord regularly (music ministry).

GUIDE TO STUDY 2

DAY 1   a) The ark of the covenant of the Lord.
b) His everlasting covenant.

DAY 2   a) His salvation, glory, marvellous deeds, greatness, worthiness, creativity, splendour, majesty, strength, joy, holiness and love.
b) Personal.

DAY 3   a) A building, probably of cedar, like his own palace.
b) Descendants, beginning with Solomon who would build the temple, continuing on to the King of Kings, whose kingdom endures for ever.

DAY 4   a) Sincere humility before the Lord, awe at the greatness of God, adoration of Him, and a confidence in His word.
b) God's people will be His very own for ever.
David's 'house' will be established for ever.
God's name will be great for ever.
God's blessing will be on David's house for ever.

DAY 5   a) God gave David victory everywhere he went as he ruled his people doing what was just and right.
b) 'The Lord will do what is good in his sight.'

DAY 6   a) Gold shields, bronze, articles of silver, gold and bronze, and a gold crown set with precious stones.
b) He dedicated all to the Lord for the building of the temple – except crown, which he wore.

DAY 7 Leaders, please fill in the story of 21:1-17 briefly, if people are not with it.
a) Personal.
b) David first built an altar there to atone for his sin, and later, the temple was built on that site. (It is now the site of the Dome of the Rock mosque in Jerusalem.)

GUIDE TO STUDY 3

DAY 1 a) He provided great amounts of the materials needed for building, and he urged all the leaders to devote their hearts and souls to the work.
b) We can give of our money, talents and time to the Lord's work, with a willing heart. (2 Cor. 8:12 is worth learning by heart.)

DAY 2 a) God would grant peace in his reign, Solomon would build the temple and have a father-son relationship with the Lord.
b) That the Lord would give him discretion and understanding, so that he would keep the law of the Lord.
c) He told him to be strong and courageous and not afraid or discouraged. He had already prepared a lot for the temple and skilled workmen were available to him.

DAY 3 a) The kingdom of Israel, God's people, which was the kingdom of the Lord.
b) Because the Lord searches every heart and understands every motive behind the thoughts (v. 9).

DAY 4 a) The Holy Spirit had revealed them to David who then informed his son Solomon.
b) The Lord.
c) Personal.

DAY 5 a) He reminded them that the temple was to be the Lord's. He had given generously and he called on them to do the same (v. 5).
b) The leaders of families, officials, etc. gave willingly, freely and wholeheartedly to the work (vv. 5-9).
c) The same challenge – to give generously and cheerfully to the Lord's work.

DAY 6 a) Great, powerful, glorious, majestic, full of splendour, everlasting, exalted.
b) The Lord's.
c) Personal.

DAY 7 a) The throne of the Lord.
b) The Lord Jesus.

GUIDE TO STUDY 4

DAY 1 a) To the high place at Gibeon, where God's Tent of Meeting was.
b) To enquire of, or worship the Lord.
c) All the important men of his kingdom (v. 2).
d) One thousand animals to offer in sacrifice.

DAY 2 a) Solomon was alone with God; God appeared to him; God took the initiative and gave him a promise.
b) He asked for wisdom and knowledge to lead his people.
c) Personal.

DAY 3 a) He wanted the temple to symbolize the greatness of God (v. 5).
b) The suggestions given are: in worship, in our manner of life, in giving and in studying the Word of God. There are others.

DAY 4 a) God loves His people, He made Solomon king, He made heaven and earth, He gave Solomon wisdom.
b) Possibly because of the witness of Solomon's life.

DAY 5 a) The ark reminded the people of His promises and His everlasting covenant. It was also a symbol of God's presence.
b) The two stone tablets with God's laws written on them, manna and Aaron's rod. (See also Deut. 10:1-5.)

DAY 6 a) To worship and bring glory to God.
b) The glory of the Lord (in the form of a cloud) filled the temple.
c) That God was present and pleased with their worship.

DAY 7 a) Solomon was promised to succeed David, as the Holy Spirit was promised to come when Jesus went to heaven.
Solomon guided his people in the ways of the Lord, as the Holy Spirit does. Solomon interceded for the people. (See also the rest of ch. 6.)
b) Solomon sits on the THRONE, and he has built the TEMPLE, just as God promised.

GUIDE TO STUDY 5

DAY 1 a) He is unique, loving, keeps His promises and is greater than the heavens.
b) Yes, Jesus God's Son, came and lived on earth. (Solomon would have expected the answer to have been 'no'.)

DAY 2 a) When a man wrongs his neighbour; when Israel has been defeated by an

enemy; when there is no rain; when there is famine or plague; when a foreigner comes to pray to Israel's God; when the people go to war; when they sin against God.
b) They must turn to God and confess their sin.

DAY 3 a) God sent down fire which consumed the burnt offering and the sacrifices.
b) They were overwhelmed by His mighty power, perhaps rather afraid, but they realised that all they could do was worship Him. They also acknowledged that He was good and loving.
After the festival they were joyful and glad in heart because of the good things the Lord had done for them.

DAY 4 a) Verses 12-16 give the response in full.
b) God would uproot them from the land and reject the temple.

DAY 5 a) He sacrificed burnt offerings, kept the feasts, appointed the priests and Levites for their duties, and appointed gatekeepers.
b) To obey His commands, just as He obeyed His Father's commands. (Note that 'Love each another' is only one of His commands.)

DAY 6 a) To test Solomon with hard questions.
b) She was overwhelmed, as his wisdom had far exceeded the reports she had heard. She realised that such a wise king must make his people happy.
c) She praised God, and acknowledged that He had put Solomon on the throne to maintain justice and righteousness.

DAY 7 a) Extremely wealthy.
b) His wealth must have enriched his people too, at least in Jerusalem.
c) Because Christ has all the treasures of wisdom and knowledge, He can enrich all His people with them.

GUIDE TO STUDY 6

DAY 1 a) Solomon. David.
b) He was an outstanding worker for Solomon. He received a prophecy through Ahijah, that he would rule ten of the tribes of Israel. He fled to Egypt to escape Solomon.

DAY 2 a) To make the people's burdens even heavier. (He accepted the advice of the younger men.)
b) Yes. Although it is true that Solomon had sinned, and prophesied, Rehoboam still had the responsibility of trying to keep the people together, and he failed miserably. So, each one of us is responsible to God for our actions, whatever the circumstances (Rom. 14:12).

DAY 3   a) To fight against the tribes which had rebelled, in order to regain the kingdom.
b) The priests, Levites, and any who sincerely loved the Lord (v. 16) sided with Rehoboam, while Jeroboam brought in goat and calf idols.

DAY 4   a) Because Rehoboam and his people had been unfaithful to the Lord.
b) They humbled themselves and admitted their sin.
c) Jerusalem was not destroyed, but its treasures were looted and the people were subjected to a foreign power.

DAY 5   a) Jeroboam rebelled; they planned to fight against the rightful king; they drove out the priests.
b) God would give Jesus the throne of David, and His kingdom would never end.

DAY 6   a) That they had not (like the northern kingdom) forsaken the Lord, but that they still worship Him as He had commanded.
b) Verse 12.
c) Personal

DAY 7   a) Jeroboam's army.
b) Abijah's army cried out to the Lord, and He routed the enemy. (Note that it was God who delivered the enemy into their hands.)

GUIDE TO STUDY 7

DAY 1   a) He did what was good and right in the eyes of his God.
b) Personal.
c) Verse 2: As HIS God (personal). Verse 4: As the God of THEIR fathers (historic). Verse 7: As OUR God (corporate).

DAY 2   a) He found himself up against an army vastly superior to his – 'a vast army', 'a million men' (other versions) – and 300 chariots, while his army consisted of 300,000 heavily armed and 280,000 lightly armed units. (Note that 'thousand' may simply mean 'unit' or 'contingent'.)
b) Personal.
c) Personal.

DAY 3   a) The Spirit of God had come upon him.
b) If you seek the Lord in earnest, you will find Him.
c) Verse 2. Personal. (Note that this is an ongoing promise, even after conversion).

DAY 4   a) People from the northern kingdom (Ephraim, Manasseh and Simeon) had come.

DAY 5   b) They had seen that God was with Asa.
c) Verse 15. They had indeed sought God eagerly, and found Him.

DAY 5   a) He deposed Maacah and cut down the idol she had made.
b) 'His heart was fully committed to the Lord.' 'The heart of King Asa was perfect before God' (LB). 'He remained faithful to the Lord' (GNB). 'The heart of Asa was blameless' (RSV).
c) Personal.

DAY 6   He bribed the king of Aram (Syria) with gold and silver out of the temple.

DAY 7   a) Of relying on the king of Aram, and not relying on God.
b) Personal.

GUIDE TO STUDY 8

DAY 1   a) He walked in the ways of David and followed the Lord's commands, and his heart was devoted to the ways of the Lord. He removed the idols and sent teachers throughout the land to teach people God's law.
b) He stationed troops in the cities and ensured that Jerusalem was protected.

DAY 2   a) He did more evil in the sight of the Lord than any before him. (He was the king that Elijah confronted.)
b) He allied himself with Ahab by marriage; he went to visit him; he agreed to join him in war. (Note that these are progressive steps in the relationship, each one a further step downward.)

DAY 3   a) When Jehoshaphat cried out to God, He helped him by drawing the attackers away from him and making them realize he was not Ahab. Can you see how Ahab's 'accidental' death must have been caused by God too?
b) For helping an ungodly king. (This came about really because he couldn't say 'no'.)

DAY 4   a) He travelled regularly among them, right through the land, to call the people back to the Lord, and he appointed judges to hear disputes.
b) To fear the Lord and be careful in pronouncing judgment, and to remember that they were acting on the Lord's authority.

DAY 5   a) He urgently turned to the Lord for help and proclaimed a fast.
b) Whole families came together to seek the Lord's help.
c) 'We do not know what to do, but our eyes are upon you' (v. 12).

DAY 6   a) That the battle was not theirs, but the Lord's, and they would not have to fight.

DAY 7   b) They fell down and worshipped, and some praised the Lord with a loud voice.

DAY 7   a) He reminded the people to trust the Lord, and he appointed singers to lead the people in singing praises to God.
b) They got together and praised the Lord in the valley, and then returned to the temple where they went on praising Him.

GUIDE TO STUDY 9

DAY 1   a) Because He had made a covenant with David to establish his kingdom for ever (1 Chron. 17:11-14).
b) He lost all his family, except one son, when enemies invaded, and he died in great pain.

DAY 2   a) His mother encouraged him to do wrong, and his advisors were those of the house of Ahab, whose ways were in direct opposition to the ways of the Lord.
b) She proceeded to murder all the royal family (her grandsons).
c) Jehosheba, sister of the king who had just been killed, and wife of a priest, hid one of the sons, Joash, and saved his life. (A picture in a Bible story book may be useful here to bring the story to life.)

DAY 3   a) He brought the young Joash out of hiding, called together the heads of the families and showed how God had preserved the king's son. Then they crowned him king at the temple.
b) Jehoiada brought back God's covenant promises to His people and had God's blessing during his long life.
c) She was shown to be a traitor and put to death.

DAY 4   a) He had a chest made and placed at the gate of the temple.
b) Gladly and generously (compare 2 Cor. 9:7).

DAY 5   a) God warned them and then brought judgment on them.
b) They plotted against him and killed him.

DAY 6   a) They both began their reigns as godly kings, but later turned away from following the Lord.
b) God gave Isaiah a vision of Himself on the throne, before He called him to be a prophet.

DAY 7   a) He did what was right in the eyes of the Lord, and he walked steadfastly before the Lord his God. He grew powerful.
b) Jehoshaphat.

c) Jehoshaphat and Jotham both 'rested' with their fathers. Jehoram – died in pain with disease; Ahaziah – murdered; Joash – killed in his bed; Amaziah – pursued and killed; Uzziah – died a leper.

GUIDE TO STUDY 10

DAY 1 a) They had used excessive rage in battle and had captured their own kinsmen (from Judah and Jerusalem), and were planning to make them slaves.
b) *Chronicles*
People of Jerusalem (Judah) were attacked. Taken as captives, naked, plundered.
Enemies (people of Samaria) showed kindness.
Healing balm given.
Weak people put on donkeys.
Taken back to Jericho.

Parable
A man travelling from Jerusalem was attacked, beaten, robbed and stripped.
A Samaritan (hated by the Jews) showed kindness, bandaged his wounds, poured in oil, put him on his own donkey and took him to Jericho.

DAY 2 a) He opened the doors of the temple and organized people to clean it. He planned to make a covenant with the Lord.
b) First, to consecrate themselves; then, to purify the temple of everything unclean.

DAY 3 a) Worship and sacrifice.
b) They rejoiced not only at what God had done for the people, but also because it had been done so quickly.

DAY 4 a) He invited the people from both kingdoms, Israel and Judah, to come together to celebrate the Passover.
b) The king of Assyria had taken captive many of the people of Israel, and deported them to Assyria.

DAY 5 a) Some scorned and ridiculed them, but some humbled themselves and came to Jerusalem.
b) There was great joy, people were blessed, and God heard their prayers.

DAY 6 a) They brought a tithe (one tenth) of everything.
b) The people gave generously and cheerfully.

DAY 7 a) He reminded them that God's power with His people was much greater than the power of the enemy. (Refer also to 2 Kgs. 6:16.)
b) He and Isaiah the prophet immediately cried out to the Lord.

GUIDE TO STUDY 11

DAY 1 a) God is angry when a person rejects His ways, and rejects even His warnings. God will punish sin. But He is long-suffering and ready to forgive if that person genuinely humbles himself and turns back to Him.
b) He did evil in the eyes of the Lord, but did not humble himself.

DAY 2 a) He repaired the temple.
b) From all the remaining people in Israel (northern kingdom) as well as from the people of Judah (southern kingdom).

DAY 3 a) Because when the Book of the Law was read, he realized that the kings before him had not kept the word of the Lord, and God must be very angry.
b) Worship God with sacrifices, in the place He has chosen.
The king is to make a copy of the Law and observe it all the days of his life.

DAY 4 a) Because his heart was responsive, and he humbled himself before God.
b) He renewed the covenant with the Lord and made the people pledge themselves to it as well.

DAY 5 a) A variety of answers, e.g. the Lord had commanded these things; to get back to the original commands, etc.
b) Jesus' teachings and the rest of the New Testament.

DAY 6 a) The king of Egypt carried him off to Egypt.
The king of Babylon prepared to take him to Babylon (but he died).
Was called to Babylon along with articles from the temple.
b) Utterly evil.

DAY 7 a) 'I tried again and again to bring the people back to me, but they refused. I had to use the Babylonians to bring punishment on them, so I handed them over to Nebuchadnezzar.'
b) God through Jeremiah prophesied that after seventy years they would return to their own land.

THE WORD WORLDWIDE

We first heard of WORD WORLDWIDE over 20 years ago when Marie Dinnen, its founder, shared excitedly about the wonderful way ministry to one needy woman had exploded to touch many lives. It was great to see the Word of God being made central in the lives of thousands of men and women, then to witness the life-changing results of them applying the Word to their circumstances. Over the years the vision for WORD WORLDWIDE has not dimmed in the hearts of those who are involved in this ministry. God is still at work through His Word and in today's self-seeking society, the Word is even more relevant to those who desire true meaning and purpose in life. WORD WORLDWIDE is a ministry of WEC International, an interdenominational missionary society, whose sole purpose is to see Christ known, loved and worshipped by all, particularly those who have yet to hear of His wonderful name. This ministry is a vital part of our work and we warmly recommend the WORD WORLDWIDE 'Geared for Growth' Bible studies to you. We know that as you study His Word you will be enriched in your personal walk with Christ. It is our hope that as you are blessed through these studies, you will find opportunities to help others discover a personal relationship with Jesus. As a mission we would encourage you to work with us to make Christ known to the ends of the earth.

Stewart and Jean Moulds – British Directors, **WEC International**.

A full list of over 50 'Geared for Growth' studies can be obtained from:

ENGLAND *North East/South*: John and Ann Edwards
5 Louvaine Terrace, Hetton-le-Hole, Tyne & Wear, DH5 9PP
Tel. 0191 5262803 Email: rhysjohn.edwards@virgin.net
North West/Midlands: Anne Jenkins
2 Windermere Road, Carnforth, Lancs., LA5 9AR
Tel. 01524 734797 Email: anne@jenkins.abelgratis.com
West: Pam Riches Tel. 01594 834241

IRELAND Steffney Preston
33 Harcourts Hill, Portadown, Craigavon, N. Ireland, BT62 3RE
Tel. 028 3833 7844 Email: sa.preston@talk21.com

SCOTLAND Margaret Halliday
10 Douglas Drive, Newton Mearns, Glasgow, G77 6HR
Tel. 0141 639 8695 Email: mhalliday@onetel.net.uk

WALES William and Eirian Edwards
Penlan Uchaf, Carmarthen Road, Kidwelly, Carms., SA17 5AF
Tel. 01554 890423 Email: penlanuchaf@fwi.co.uk

UK CO-ORDINATOR
Anne Jenkins
2 Windermere Road, Carnforth, Lancs., LA5 9AR
Tel. 01524 734797 Email: anne@jenkins.abelgratis.com

UK Website: www.gearedforgrowth.co.uk

Christian Focus Publications
publishes books for all ages

Our mission statement –

STAYING FAITHFUL

In dependence upon God we seek to help make His infallible word, the Bible, relevant. Our aim is to ensure that the Lord Jesus Christ is presented as the only hope to obtain forgiveness of sin, live a useful life and look forward to heaven with Him.

REACHING OUT

Christ's last command requires us to reach out to our world with His gospel. We seek to help fulfill that by publishing books that point people towards Jesus and help them develop a Christ-like maturity. We aim to equip all levels of readers for life, work, ministry and mission.

Books in our adult range are published in three imprints.

Christian Focus contains popular works including biographies, commentaries, basic doctrine, and Christian living. Our children's books are also published in this imprint.

Mentor focuses on books written at a level suitable for Bible College and seminary students, pastors, and other serious readers; the imprint includes commentaries, doctrinal studies, examination of current issues, and church history.

Christian Heritage contains classic writings from the past.